TALES FROM RUMI

Mathnawi Selections for Young Readers

TALES FROM RUMI

Mathnawi Selections for Young Readers

Edited by Ali Fuat Bilkan

New Jersey

Published by Tughra Books
345 Clifton Ave., Clifton,
NJ, 07011, USA

www.tughrabooks.com

Art Director Engin Çiftçi
Illustrations by Erdinç Şemen
Translated by Jeannette Squires Okur

Library of Congress Cataloging-in-Publication Data is available

ISBN: 978-1-59784-124-5

Printed by

İmak Ofset, Istanbul - Turkey
Certificate : 12531
Phone : +90 212 656 49 97

Contents

Preface

The fables in this collection have been selected and abridged from the *Mathnawi*. The *Mathnawi* is a literary masterpiece that was composed by Mawlana Jalaladdin Rumi, a great Sufi master of the thirteenth century and one of the most published poets in the West today. It is one of the cornerstones of Middle Eastern, Central and South Asian culture. The *Mathnawi* was a call for unity and virtue in a world full of conflict, wars and migrations. It emphasizes human virtue and the development of the spiritual insight of the heart.

The manner in which events and situations are interpreted in the stories reflects a strong, lively cultural and literary heritage of the East. At the end of every tale, the writer addresses his own heart, drawing attention to just some of the wisdom which can be gained from the fable, but readers may find much more. Young people and adults will read these tales with special delight and learn new ways of looking at the world.

The Rabbit and the Lion

The herd of wild animals that had come to graze in the beautiful meadow did so crouched down in fear of a lion. Indeed, a lion often laid an ambush in this meadow, snatching up and carrying away one of the animals. So, the fertile pasture was spoiled for them. The poor animals wracked their brains until at last they went to the lion and offered to bring him anything he wanted to eat, as long as he would not touch them. However, the lion, wise in the ways of the world, realized that they might be laying a trap for him and did not accept their offer. "I prefer to earn my own living," he said.

The animals swore to be true to their word and finally succeeded in convincing the lion. According to their agreement, the lion's portion was to be brought before him each day without any trouble. The animals would draw lots to determine which one of them was to become the lion's meal so that the others could graze in peace. One day, the rabbit drew the lot and so it was known that he would be sent to the lion. At this, the rabbit protested, crying, "How long will this oppression last?"

The other wild animals urged the rabbit, "All this time we've remained true to our word and sacrificed our own lives. Don't you dare act stubbornly and ruin our good name! Get going so the lion won't be insulted!" The rabbit pleaded with his friends for a little more time. "I have a plan," he said to them, "that could save both my life and yours." Although the other animals insisted, they were not able to find out what the rabbit intended to do.

The rabbit headed toward where the lion lived and arrived just a little late. Upon seeing his prey come late, the lion roared violently and clawed the earth. He was thinking that he was wrong to have made a deal with the animals. Besides, this rabbit was heading toward him with very slow hops. The lion steamed up and boiled over with anger as he watched the rabbit coming from far away. Seeing the rabbit's relaxed demeanor, he exploded. "Just who do you think you are? I've torn apart elephants, not to mention a thousand or so rabbits," he roared.

The rabbit begged the lion to forgive him and offered his excuse: "Honestly, my lord. I set out early this morning. With another rabbit as my companion, I was hurrying to your presence, when along the way, we were attacked by another lion. I begged and pleaded. 'Don't kill us. We are slaves of the King of kings,' I said. 'Who is that king?' the strange lion replied. 'I'll tear him to pieces.'

'Just let me see my king one last time and I'll tell him about you,' I said. 'If you leave your friend as a hostage, I'll let you go,' the strange lion replied. All my begging and pleading was useless; he took my friend and let me go. Of course, my friend is very attractive and also two times plumper than I am."

The hungry lion, enraged by this news, commanded the rabbit to show him the enemy who had trespassed on his preserves. He said, "If you're telling the truth, then lead me there, and let's give that lion his due. But if you're lying, I'll punish you." The rabbit led the way, hoping to draw the lion into the trap he had laid for him. Soon, they came to the top of a deep well. The rabbit said, "Look, there they are, both of them," and he pointed into the well.

As he approached the well, the lion noticed that the rabbit had hopped backwards. "Why did you hop back?" he asked. "Don't stay back there. Get in front of me!"

"Don't you see that I'm trembling? My paws are shaking and my heart is in my throat," replied the rabbit. The lion told the rabbit to look into the well and see if the lion he had met was there or not. The rabbit said, "If you hold me in your lap, then I'll be able to look."

As the lion took the rabbit onto his lap and leaned over to look into the well, he saw another lion and a fat rabbit there. Thinking that he saw his enemy in the water, he pushed the rabbit from his lap and leapt into the well. When the lion jumped onto his own reflection in the water, he was unable to climb out of the well again and drowned.

The rabbit, who had managed to get rid of the lion by deceiving him into his trap, bounced up and down with glee and immediately hopped back to his friends to tell them the good news. All of the animals joyfully hugged the rabbit, congratulated him and thanked him for saving their lives.

Know this: The lion possessed power and courage but lacked wisdom. So, the rabbit was able to outwit the lion, whose end came about because he did not use his reason well. The reason of man is like a boundless ocean, and you must be a good diver in order not to get drowned in it like the lion. A powerful body always needs a powerful mind.

The Merchant and the Parrot

Once upon a time, a rich merchant had a most wonderful parrot. Everybody admired her for her bright feathers and her beautiful voice. The parrot enjoyed all the admiration, but the poor creature was very unhappy about the life she led imprisoned in her cage. A day came when the merchant was going to India to trade. Before he left, he asked his friends and servants what gifts they would like him to bring back. Each person asked him to bring one gift and to fulfill one wish.

When it was the parrot's turn, the generous merchant said to her, "Tell me, what shall I bring you?" The parrot replied, "Please tell all the parrots there about me and give them my greetings. Ask them if it is fair that they live happily and freely among the trees and cliffs while I'm exiled to a cage here. Tell them I want their help."

The merchant promised that he would say this to the parrots in India and set out on his journey. When he arrived in India after a long and arduous passage, he saw some parrots in the tops of the trees in a meadow. He halted his horse, approached the parrots, calling to them, and told them what his parrot had said. Suddenly, one of the parrots fell trembling to the ground and died. The man, distressed that he had been the cause of the poor creature's death, regretted what he had done. "Maybe it was one of my parrot's relatives," he thought to himself.

Several weeks later, the merchant completed his trading in India and returned to his homeland. He distributed the gifts he had brought one by one and also made donations to charity in thanksgiving for his safe return. Around the same time, the merchant's beautiful parrot asked him what he had seen and heard there pertaining to her own situation.

Even though the merchant said that he was very upset about what he had done and that he did not want to tell what had happened, the parrot insisted on hearing it. Then the merchant confessed, "I repeated what you'd said to the parrots I met there, but one of them was badly frightened and dropped dead." The merchant added that he was sorry to have been the cause of that parrot's death and that he very much regretted having said anything.

When the merchant's parrot heard how the bird in India had died, she straightaway fell trembling to the bottom of her cage and froze rigid like stone. Witnessing this, the merchant leapt up and threw his hat to the ground. Then, he flung himself to the ground next to the cage, filled with grief at having lost his beautiful bird.

After weeping for a while, hopelessly, the merchant removed the dead bird from her cage and placed her on the ground beside him. In an instant, the parrot woke up, shook her wonderful feathers and flew up to a high tree

branch. The merchant was astonished at this and exclaimed, "O bird, explain yourself so that I can understand what happened. What did the bird in India do to make you lay this trap for me, to make you hurt me?"

The parrot answered the merchant in this way: "In doing what he did, the bird in India gave me advice. By pretending to be dead, he sent me the message to behave in the same way, implying, 'If you want to be rescued from your cage, do as I did. As you see, I died and I am free.'"

When the merchant heard this reply, he understood what had really happened and learned an important lesson from the conduct of this bird, who bade him a fond farewell as she flew away.

⟨⟩❖⟨⟩

Know this:

When Spring comes do rocks turn green?

You, too, be modest like the earth and let colorful roses grow from you.

Your desire for the admiration of others keeps you caged.

The Grocer and the Parrot

Once, a grocer had a talkative, green parrot with a beautiful voice. The parrot stayed in the grocer's shop all day long, entertaining the customers with delightful words and jokes. The parrot, who knew how to speak with people just like a human, was also an expert at chirping melodies. One day, the grocer had to leave his shop for a short while to go on an errand. As the parrot was flitting about on its own in the shop, it suddenly knocked over a huge bottle of rose oil. What did the grocer behold when he returned to the shop? All was in disarray and everything in the shop was splattered with rose oil.

The grocer's own robe was also stained with rose oil. Angered by the parrot's naughty

antics, the grocer slapped the bird on the head. The parrot was very upset by this blow, and soon after, it began to lose its feathers. Then, the parrot became silent and withdrawn and began to observe its master sadly from a corner. When the grocer saw this, he felt sorry that he had hurt the poor creature and regretted a thousand times over what he had done. But in vain!

The grocer, who soon thereafter watched his parrot lose the last of its beautiful feathers and remain bald, was left stroking his beard, mumbling, "If only my hand had been broken so I wouldn't have struck such a fine-tongued creature." The grocer began to shower alms on the poor and helped many others in hopes that his bird might come to its senses and speak again. Three days and three nights passed with the grocer sitting dejectedly in his shop. However, at the same time he went on chatting with the parrot, hoping that his foolish banter might encourage it to speak again. Just then, a man without a single hair on his head came in from the street.

Breaking its long silence, the parrot suddenly began to squawk with excitement, "Hey, baldy! Look at me! Did you knock over a bottle of rose oil, too?"

All the passers-by who heard this began to laugh. The parrot apparently believed that this ascetic, a man who had donned a vest and shaved his head for spiritual reasons, was bald because he had spilled a bottle of rose oil and been slapped by his master, just like the parrot!

Know this: The eyes of the parrot saw only the physical surface of things and were not able to discern what the spiritual or inner eye perceives. So, it likened the bald man to itself. The passers-by smiled at the assumption of the parrot that only saw what it wanted to see through its sensual eyes. True knowledge is acquired by the heart and not through sensual perception. Observe the hundreds of thousands of things that resemble one another and take note of the seventy kinds of difference among them.

The Lion Tattoo

Long ago, it was a common custom to have a tattoo. Those who had various images and designs drawn on their hands, feet and shoulders would moan and groan at the pain caused by the needle which made the blue tattoos.

One day, a man wanting a tattoo on his shoulder said to the tattooist, "Give me a tattoo gently, without hurting me." The tattooist asked, "Young man, what image would you like me to prick onto your skin?"

"Draw a roaring lion, because my birth sign is Leo!" said the young man. "But make it a handsome lion."

"Where would you like the tattoo?" asked the tattooist. "On my shoulder blade," answered the young man.

As soon as the tattooist made the first jab of the needle into the young man's shoulder, he screamed. His shoulder shrank from the stab of the needle. Reeling in pain, the young man said to the tattooist, "Master, you're killing me! Tell me what picture you're drawing."

"A lion," the tattooist replied, "just as you ordered." Still smarting from the pain, the young man asked, "Which part of the lion are you drawing right now?"

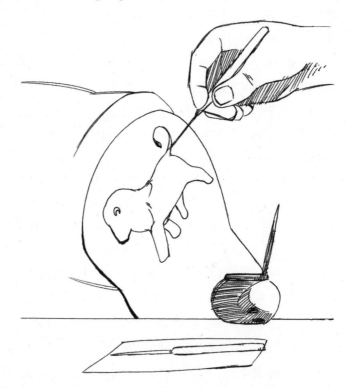

"I have just started drawing the tip of its tail," said the tattooist. "Oh good heavens, forget the tail!" exclaimed the young man. "The pain of the lion's tail hurts so much I'm about to faint. Why don't you draw a lion with no tail?"

The tattooist stopped drawing the lion's tail, and without paying any attention to the moans and groans, started to prick out another part of the lion on the young man's shoulder. Wincing, the young man asked again which part of the lion he was drawing. "I'm drawing its ear," answered the tattooist. Doubling over in pain, the man cried, "O master, stop! Don't let the lion have ears."

Upon hearing this, the tattooist stopped in the middle of his work and began to work with his needle on another part of the shoulder blade. The man soon asked again, "Now what limb are you drawing?"

"I'm drawing the lion's stomach," said the tattooist. Unable to stand the stab of the needle, the man cried impatiently, "Stop! Don't let the lion have a stomach! What does it need a stomach for?"

At this, the tattooist was totally bewildered. He stood a long time with his fingers in his mouth. Refusing to go any further, he threw his needle angrily to the ground and yelled, "Has anybody in this world ever seen a lion with no tail, no head and no stomach? It is like no lion God ever created!"

Know this: In order to have the right to wear the sign of the lion, the bravest and most majestic of animals, you have to prove your courage, patience, and surrender to the will of your Maker. The purpose of human existence can only be fulfilled by those who overcome their lower selves. How can the lower self be tested without pain? How can virtues be proved except in the whirlwind of trouble? All the ordeals that are sent to us are sent for our transformation.

The Lion's Share

Once, a lion, a wolf and a fox set out to hunt. The animals, who had agreed to help one another, were planning to catch tasty game together in the high meadow.

Even though the male lion was embarrassed to be seen hunting with a wolf and a fox, he had agreed to accompany them out of necessity. As the lion, wolf and fox traveled over hills and streams, they caught a mountain ox, a goat and a fat rabbit. They dragged their prey down from the mountain and carried it to the edge of a wood.

The wolf and the fox eyed the game hungrily and waited for the sultan of sultans, the lion, to have them divide the game fairly. The lion saw their impatience and, thinking of the trick he was going to play on them, smiled slyly. The lion said to the wolf, "O wolf, come and divide these." The wolf said, "Sultan, let the wild ox be your share, since it is big and you are great, fleshy and swift. Let the goat be mine, since it is middle-sized game. And let the fox have the rabbit."

As soon as the wolf finished his sentence, the lion roared with great rage, and with one paw, tore apart that ignorant animal who, not knowing his place, had presumed to talk of "I" and "you," and "my share" and "your share" when all belonged of right to the lion.

Then, turning to the fox, the lion said, "Come on. You divide these for our meal." The fox bowed respectfully in front of the lion and said, "O distinguished Sultan, let this fat ox be your breakfast, let the goat be your lunch,

and let the rabbit be your starter for your evening meal!"

At this, the lion said, "How nice, you have divided them fairly. Tell me, who did you learn this from?" The fox replied, "O Sultan of the World, I learned this from the fate of the wolf you just tore to shreds." Upon hearing this, the lion was pleased by the fox's modest manner and rewarded him with a generous gift.

Know this: Learning from the mistakes of his fellow, the fox said the whole should be the portion of the lion. By not presuming to divide the prey of the lion king, the fox acknowledged the absolute authority of the King, and thus he not only saved his life but also received a generous gift.

The Deaf Man Visits His Ill Neighbor

One day, a man who knew the right way to behave in the world advised a deaf man that one of his neighbors was ill and that he absolutely must visit him. The deaf man replied, "I am hard of hearing. If I go and see him, what can I say to him? Especially if he's really ill, then his voice won't be clear, and I'll never be able to understand what he says."

Nevertheless, he decided to do his duty and visit the sick man. While on his way, he thought to himself, "When the patient moves his lips, I'll be able to guess what he's saying. 'How are you, O troubled friend?' I'll say. Of course, he'll reply, 'I'm fine,' or 'I'm well.' 'Thanks be to God,' I'll say. After that I'll ask, 'What have you eaten?' He'll reply, 'I've had a sherbet drink,' or

'lentil soup.' I'll say, 'To your health, bon appétit.' Then, 'Which doctor is looking after you?'
I'll ask. Whatever his answer, I'll say, 'He's one
who brings great fortune with him. If he sees
you, you will get better.' And 'We tried him,
too. Wherever he goes, people get what they
need from him,' I'll add."

The deaf man, who arrived at the sick
man's house with these thoughts, began to ask
questions one after the other, and interpreting
the answers as he had guessed, responded to
them in the way in which he had previously
prepared. "How are you, friend?"

"Don't ask! I'm dying."

"Oh, thanks be to God!" The patient was
insulted by these words, lost his morale and
became upset. "What reason has he got for
being thankful? It must mean that this man
wants only the worst for me," he muttered.

The man who could not hear asked, "What
have you eaten?" The sick man replied angrily,
"Poison!" When, without hearing the answer,
the visitor exclaimed, "Bon appétit," the sick
man's distress increased.

After this the visitor asked, "Which doctor
is coming to find a cure for your troubles?" The

sick man rebuked him, saying, "The Angel of Death is coming. What's it to you? Get out of my house and look after your own business!" The man replied, "You should be happy. His coming is very blessed." The sick man was really disconcerted by this reply and thought, "It seems like this man is my mortal enemy."

However, his clueless deaf neighbor returned home, pleased at having done his duty and visited a sick friend.

❧

Know this: The sick man was quick to jump to the false conclusion that the visitor was a mortal enemy who wanted to see him weak, but the deaf man was pleased he had visited his neighbor, thinking he had done his duty. It is not enough to understand only what you hear with your ears. It is important to understand some things with your heart, which senses hidden meanings.

The Chinese Painters and the Anatolian Artists

Once upon a time, some Chinese painters and some Anatolian artists were arguing as to who were the better artists. The country's sultan decided to settle the dispute with an exhibition of their skills. He called both groups of artists into his presence and commanded them to take part in a competition to show proof of their art. "In order to understand which of your claims is true, I am going to test you," the sultan declared. The Chinese painters said to the Sultan, "Then give us a room in which to paint. And give the Anatolian artists a room, too."

The Chinese took one of two rooms facing each other; and the Anatolian artists settled into the other. A curtain was drawn between the two rooms and the artists began to work.

The Chinese requested one hundred different colors of paint from the sultan. The sultan immediately fulfilled their wish. The Anatolian artists, on the other hand, used no colors at all and said, "Neither pictures, nor paint are of use. What's important is first to clean up all the dirt." Behind the curtain, they began to cleanse their room from all filth and contented themselves with polishing all the room's walls.

Days passed by. The Anatolian artists' room became as clear and bright as the sky. Meanwhile, the Chinese, who had requested various paints every day and painted colorful scenes, finished their art and, in high spirits, started to celebrate. The Chinese artists informed the sultan they had finished and threw their doors wide to let him see their magnificent work in hundreds of subtle colors. The sultan marveled at the fascinating beauty of their wall paintings.

Then, he entered Anatolian artists' room opposite. The walls of the room were completely bare. When the sultan saw the empty walls, he was taken aback. However, when the Anatolian artists removed the curtain separating their room from that of the Chinese, all the paintings on the opposite wall were suddenly reflected onto their polished wall. The sultan saw all the paintings he had seen in the room of the Chinese artists, only here they were shinier and more animated. The reflection, with the sunlight playing and dancing on it, made the manifold variety of the Chinese colors more delicate and beautiful.

Amazed by the artistry he saw, the sultan said, "Of course, these paintings are more beautiful and alluring," and he declared the Anatolian artists the winners of the competition.

Know this: The walls are like the heart. It must be purified like an unspotted mirror which takes and reflects infinite images. If the heart is pure, it can receive an endless variety of shades and hues. Then, its true nature, in all its spaciousness and fullness, will shine forth. Those who polish their hearts are saved from smell and color. They witness beauty with every breath without pause.

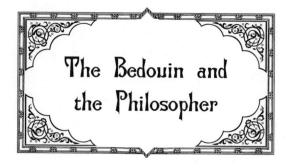

The Bedouin and the Philosopher

One morning, a desert Bedouin loaded two big sacks onto his camel and set out on his way. He was perched between the two sacks, swaying back and forth, when he came across a philosopher walking in the sand. The philosopher, puffed with pride, began to converse with the Bedouin by asking him where he was from, what he did for a living, and so on.

The philosopher asked the Bedouin, "What's in those sacks you're carrying?" The Bedouin replied, "There's wheat in one of them and sand in the other, nothing a person could eat." The philosopher laughed derisively. "Why did you load sand onto your camel?" he scoffed. "Because there's wheat in one of the sacks. I filled the other one with sand so they'd be balanced," the Bedouin replied.

The philosopher belittled him. "If you had an ounce of sense, you would have put half of the wheat in one sack and half in the other. That way you would have lightened the sacks and the camel's load." The Bedouin, who had not thought of this, was so struck by the philosopher's sagacity that he conceived a great respect for him.

He was, however, curious about something, too. How was it that such an intelligent, knowledgeable person was traveling poorly clothed and on foot in a vast desert like this, subject to countless difficulties? The Bedouin, who pitied the philosopher, had him mount his camel and asked him the questions on his mind. "O wise man, tell me a little about yourself! How did a smart person like you end up like this? Or are you a vizier or sultan who has disguised himself to mingle among commoners?"

The philosopher replied, "Don't judge me by my clothes or my appearance. I am neither of those. I'm just a simple, common man."

"How many camels do you have? How many oxen?" asked the Bedouin curiously. "Don't press me any more. I don't have any camels or oxen," said the philosopher. "Well then, do you own a store or any property?" asked the Bedouin.

"What store, what property?" replied the philosopher. The Bedouin said, "Well then, let me ask you about your money and assets. Certainly a person who possesses such profound knowledge must also know how to turn the world's copper into gold."

"I swear to you, all my savings are not even enough to pay for one night's dinner. I just keep wandering around in rags with a few pennies in my pocket. I go wherever someone will give me a piece of bread. All that this knowledge and talent have brought me are pipedreams and headaches," replied the philosopher.

The Bedouin, on hearing these words, kicked the philosopher off his camel. "Make use of your knowledge!" he said and advised him to work and earn his way in the world.

❦

Know this: Knowledge that is not applied to life but remains only in words and ideas is useless, like a heavy burden of sand. If knowledge and practice are joined together, they become beneficial. You should treat everyone with respect and take lessons from ordinary people, no matter how much you think you know. True wisdom opens a door for you.

The Mouse and the Camel

One fine day, a tiny mouse took a giant camel's halter into his paw. Thinking himself the camel's driver, he strutted along, his chest swelling with pride. While the camel continued calmly on her way, as is her nature and custom, the mouse kept praising himself. "What a brave young hero I am!" he exclaimed. The camel, who had noticed how the mouse was boasting, prepared to teach him a good lesson.

Some time later, the mouse and the camel came to a wide river that not even an elephant would be able to cross. The mouse stood on the river bank, puzzled as to what to do. The camel scolded the mouse, "You have been my companion through the mountains and des-

ert. Why have you stopped? Why are you so
surprised? Plunge into the water like a man!
Continue guiding me into the river. Don't give
up half way!"

"This water is really wide and very deep," answered the mouse. "O, companion, I'm afraid of drowning."

"Wait a minute. Let's see how deep the water is," said the camel.

She dipped her hoof into the water, turned and said to the mouse, "O, you blind mouse, the water is only up to the knee. There's no need to get butterflies over it!"

"O camel, what looks like an ant to you is a dragon to me. There's a difference between knees. The water only comes to your knee, but it's deep enough to be over my head," said the mouse.

So that the mouse might learn his place and a good lesson, the camel said, "If that's so, then quit being so insolent and don't try to look like more than you are! See to it that you compete with mice your own size. Don't try to measure up to camels!"

The mouse, embarrassed by his behavior, vowed not to repeat it. He begged the camel, "For God's sake, please take me across this treacherous water!" The camel, taking pity on the mouse, replied, "Come on. Hop on. Sit on my hump and I'll take you to the opposite bank.

Crossing this river is my job alone. I've taken many greater than you over this water." And taking the mouse onto her back, she passed across the river.

❦

Know this: The camel reminded the boastful mouse if you imitate those who are more powerful or able than you, it can lead to great problems on the journey of life and that safe passage depends on recognizing your own characteristics. If you are not the ruler, be a simple subject! If you are not the captain, do not try to steer the ship.

The Grape Fight

Once upon a time, a man gave an Iranian, an Arab, a Turk and a Greek whom he saw together one gold coin between them. In doing them this kindness, he said, "Buy whatever you like with this money."

One of the four, the Iranian, said, "I'm going to buy *angur* with it." The Arab disagreed. "You fool! I don't want *angur*. I want *inab*." The third person, the Turk, did not like either of those ideas. "I don't want *angur* or *inab*. I'm going to buy *üzüm*," he said. The Greek, who had been watching what was going on, cried, "Stop this foolishness. I want *astaphil*. I'm going to buy *astaphil* with this money!"

At once, all four of them started arguing, each man yelling that what he wanted should be bought. Fists flew and, fighting hard, they were soon beating each other up. Before long, a wise man who was passing by intervened in the fight and asked what their problem was.

The Iranian said, "I want to buy *angur* with the money we were given." "No, we're going to buy *inab*," protested the Arab. "I say, let's buy *üzüm*," shouted the Turk. "Neither of those. We're going to buy *astaphil* with our money," insisted the Greek.

The sage understood immediately what all four people talking in different languages actually wanted. He said, "Ah! I can fulfill the wishes of all of you with one and the same gold coin. If you honestly give me your trust, your one gold coin will become as four, and four at odds will become as one united."

Then he went and bought four bunches of grapes. Sharing the grapes between them, he

fulfilled the desires of all four. So, the senseless argument found its end.

***

Know this: People must understand each other or be lost to quarrelling. We can find similarities in our differences when we understand each other. All four men in the story, though they did not know it, desired the same thing. They finally came to know this with the help of a wise man who knew many languages. They reconciled through the tongue of mutual understanding and learnt to be one in heart which is better than to be one in tongue. Purify and unite your hearts so that no speck of dust remains between them.

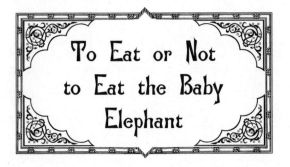

To Eat or Not to Eat the Baby Elephant

One day, a wise man came across a caravan in India which was traveling with much difficulty. The travelers' clothes were disheveled and they had no provisions. The sage, who saw that this group had been hungry and miserable for days, understood their suffering and warned them not to eat the baby elephants that they would see along the way.

"O travelers, he said, "I know that you are hungry, and I know that your hunger has made you suffer. But, for the sake of God, don't kill the baby elephants you're going to see along your way, and don't eat them! In your hearts, you may want to kill the plump, defenseless elephant calves, but don't forget that their mothers, whose trunks spit fire and smoke, are armed. They'll make you regret it if you do."

The sage warned them again and again to eat grass and leaves when hungry and not to touch the baby elephants. But the journey was long and tiring. The travelers, their stomachs cramped with hunger, were searching for something to eat, when suddenly they saw a fat, newborn elephant calf by the road.

Weak with hunger, their eyes ravenous like wolves, the travelers fell upon the calf and devoured it. One of them, however, remembered the sage's warning and, because he was afraid of inviting disaster, he did not eat the elephant and also warned his friends not to consume it.

Soon after, those who had eaten the baby elephant fell into a deep sleep. The other who had refused to eat the elephant's meat took up watch over them, remaining awake because of his hunger. It was not long before he spied an enraged elephant thundering toward them. First, the elephant sniffed the mouth of the watchman who had not eaten her calf. She could not detect any scent. The mother elephant circled around

the watchman several times but did not hurt him at all.

The mother elephant soon came to those who had eaten her calf and sniffed their mouths one by one. Their breath revealed the aroma of the baby elephant they had fried and eaten. Smelling her calf, the mother elephant ripped them all to pieces right then and there.

Know this: If you do not subdue your desires and show patience in the face of distress, such as hunger and thirst, you should be prepared for more sorrowful calamities in the future. Only one of the travelers remembers the warning and does not eat the elephant's flesh. Though it seems he might starve to death, he is saved because of his restraint, unlike his fellow travelers. O wicked one, you are eating a baby elephant. Your enemy, the adult elephant, will hunt and destroy you.

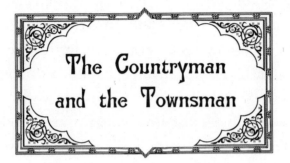

The Countryman
and the Townsman

Once upon a time, a townsman struck up a friendship with a villager. Whenever the villager came to the town, he would lodge in the townsman's house and stay for two or three months. In the mornings, he would sit in the townsman's store and use the store property as if it were his own. His friend, the townsman would shoulder all his expenses and invite him as a guest to his table.

One day, the villager said to his friend, "O sir, won't you come to our village, even if it is just to relax and rest? What's to lose? In the name of God, please come with your wife and children. Right now it is the season of roses, springtime. If you come in summer, it'll be the season of fruit. I'd like to serve you. Gather your family and friends and come. Stay in our village for three or four months. The village is beautiful in spring. All the meadows are green. The blooming tulips steal one's heart." In this way, he invited his friend to his village. In order to escape his village friend's gush of words, the townsman promised he would come one day. After he made this promise, exactly eight years passed.

The villager constantly asked his town friend, "When are you going to come? Springs and winters are whizzing by. My whole family is awaiting yours." The townsman always found excuses, saying, "This year this guest came," or "Something came up." Then he would repeat his promise, saying, "If I can finish my work, I'll come running."

The villager came every year, landed on the townsman's roof like a stork, ate, drank and lived for free on the townsman's back for months. At last, having stayed another three months in the townsman's house, he was unable to stand the embarrassment. Forcing his friend once again to promise to come to his village, he returned home. However, ten years went by, and the townsman still did not fulfill his promise.

Finally, the townsman's children begged and pleaded with their father. They convinced him to go to the village, saying, "You've given him more than his due. In order to please him, you've suffered enough troubles. He, too, wants to repay you by playing the host." At last, the townsman and his children finished their preparations and set out on the road. As they were heading toward the village on their mules, they imagined the beautiful sights awaiting them there.

After a month-long journey they finally arrived in the village. They were hungry and tired, and their animals had gone without hay and fodder. But strangely enough, their village friend seemed to be avoiding them. Pretending not to know them, he refused to open his door.

That night, when a heavy rainstorm began, the town merchant knocked on the villager's door once again and begged him for, if nothing else, a place in which he and his children could take shelter. The villager replied, "I'll give you

shelter, if you take a bow and arrow, keep watch for the wolves that will come down from the mountain and protect my herds." The poor townsman agreed to do this and, taking shelter in a hollow with his children, began to wait.

At midnight the townsman spied a pack of wolves coming down from the mountain. He took the bow in his hands, aimed at one of the wolves and shot it down with one arrow. But the villager cried in distress, "What have you done? The animal you shot was my donkey's foal!" The townsman, who was certain that the animal he had killed was a wolf, asked, "In the dark of night, in the middle of this rainstorm, how can you know that the animal I shot was your donkey's foal?" When the villager answered, "I recognized him by how he broke wind," the townsman's patience ended.

Striding up to the villager, he shouted, "You fool, if you can recognize your donkey's foal from meters away and in the middle of the night in a rainstorm, then how can you not know your friend of ten years who hosted you for months at a time?" Then he gave the villager a thorough beating and said, "Even if I shot your donkey's

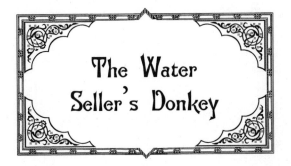

The Water Seller's Donkey

Once, there was an old water seller who owned an exhausted, emaciated donkey. The poor man barely earned a living by selling water door-to-door. For this reason, he did not have enough money to buy his donkey grain. The poor donkey, which had open wounds on its back from the heavy loads it carried, could not find any dry grass or straw, much less barley.

When the sultan's stable keeper saw the donkey's state, he felt sorry for it. "Why does this poor animal look like this?" he angrily asked his friend, the water seller. The old man replied, "Ah sir, I can barely fill my own stomach. How am I supposed to find food for my donkey?" The sultan's stable keeper said, "Give

me this donkey for a few days and let him regain his strength in the sultan's stables."

The man gave him his donkey, and the keeper took it to the sultan's stables, where he tied it up. In amazement the poor donkey watched the beautiful, supple Arabian horses, whose food in the stables was plentiful. When the donkey saw this breed of horse, which was fed with straw, barley, and many different kinds of fodder, he looked at himself and said bitterly, "O my Lord, why don't You give me these horses' comfort and lifestyle? Why is torment and trouble just for me? I can't even stand in one spot because of the painful wounds on my back. My stomach is empty. I feel wretched. Yet, they enjoy such abundance and plenty."

One morning, as the donkey was wallowing in this state of self-pity, voices shouting, "War has broken out!" were heard. The Arabian horses were saddled, bridled and made ready for battle. While the donkey trotted around alone in the stables, the horses were taking part in a fierce war.

The horses, which had been the targets of enemy arrows and spears, returned to the stables wounded, bruised and exhausted. Their hooves were bound, arrows were plucked out of their wounded bodies, their wounds were treated, and the sword and lance lacerations bandaged.

When the donkey saw the horses in this most miserable plight, some grievously wounded and others dying, he was thankful for his own state and prayed, "O Lord, I accept my poverty and hunger. It's enough that You keep me far from this difficult duty, that You don't subject me to the toils of war. I don't want lots of food and all the luxury of the world, nor do I need arrows and spears being extracted from my wounds."

Know this: One who tires of the world's nourishment and ugly wounds and wishes for salvation should abandon self-obsession and selfish desires.

The Donkey
and the Fox

Once upon a time, a lion and an elephant who lived in the same lands began to fight. The fight dragged on and, by the time it was over, the lion was wounded and exhausted. The poor lion lay in his den, covered in blood. Hungry and hopeless, he began to rest.

When the lion did not go out to hunt, it was bad news for the animals who lived mostly off the scraps of meat he left behind. The hungry animals pressured the lion to do something. The lion immediately summoned the fox and told her to find game for both himself and the animals who lived off the remains. "Go and find an ox or a donkey and trick him into coming here. That way you'll fill both my stomach and yours," said the lion to the fox.

So, the fox began to search for game, and in a barren meadow she came across a scrawny donkey. She approached him and greeted him cordially. "What are you doing in this dry, barren meadow among the rocks?" the fox asked the donkey. "Sometimes I'm oppressed with anxiety, and sometimes I'm thankful that I've discovered the destiny God gave me. There are things far worse," answered the donkey.

The fox talked as skillfully as she could in order to lure the donkey to the lion's den. She told him that he needed to make some effort if he was to seek his destiny and find better and more plentiful food. The donkey said that he was satisfied with the sustenance allotted to him, and that he was used to being patient and accepting whatever providence the Sustenance-Giver had ordained for him. The fox began to tell the donkey about lush meadows and damp pastures, "How happy the animals in that meadow are! There's so much greenery, so many meadows and fields that a camel wouldn't be caught dead there. If you continue to stay here, you'll die of starvation one day." The fox exaggerated and embellished his descriptions, dazzling the donkey's senses.

What a pity that the donkey did not think of asking the fox, "If all that is so, then why are you so thin and ugly?" Instead, he was duped by the fox's promises and decided to follow her.

The fox pulled the donkey by his beard straight to the meadow where the lion lived. The lion saw the donkey coming from far away. Without waiting for the donkey to approach, the greedy lion suddenly let out a terrible roar. Yet, the lion was not even able to budge an inch from his resting spot. The donkey leapt at the lion's roar and fled.

The fox approached the lion, muttering, "Ah, your Majesty, why didn't you wait until the donkey got close to you?" The lion replied, "For a moment, I thought I had my strength. I'm so hungry and weak that I lost my patience. I couldn't resist!"

The lion commanded the fox to go and trick the donkey and bring him there once again. The fox told the lion not to hurry the matter. Confidently, the lion said he would be able to kill the donkey easily this time. The fox approached the donkey again.

When the donkey saw the fox, he brayed, "I'd better steer clear of friends like you. What did I do to you to make you deliver me to a dragon?"

"Ah, friend, what looked to you like a lion or a dragon wasn't either. Clearly, it was magic. Look, I'm smaller than you, and nothing happened to me. If there weren't a magic spell over that kind of meadow, would it stay so green? It's a precaution being used to keep other animals from settling there," reasoned the fox. "Go away! I don't want to see you. You almost had my blood on your paws," cried the donkey.

However, the donkey's objections and his ability to escape the fox's tricks did not last long. Hunger and ambition dragged the donkey back to that green field again. This time, the donkey came much closer to the lion. Suddenly, the lion roared, pounced on the donkey's neck and tore him to pieces. Soon, the lion regained his former strength and left his dead game to drink some water.

The fox took advantage of this opportunity and swallowed the donkey's heart and liver in one gulp. When the lion returned to his den, he wanted to eat the donkey's heart and liver, but he could not find them. "What happened to the donkey's heart and liver?" the lion asked the fox. The fox, in all her cleverness, answered, "If our dear donkey, who experienced such tumult, such fright, such a leap and flight from the mountain, had had a heart or liver, would he have come here again?"

───※───

Know this: The donkey was foolish to allow himself to be deluded by the trickster fox for a second time. He prepared his own end with his insincere and false vow of repentance and by yielding to the fox's enticement again. Ambition makes a person blind and foolish; it renders people unknowledgeable and leads them easily to death.

The Bird's Advice

Once morning, a hunter laid a trap for a bird. Unknowingly, a poor sparrow got caught in it. When the hunter came to take the sparrow from the trap, the sparrow addressed him, saying, "O, great one, you have killed giant oxen, sheep and camels, yet you've never managed to fill your belly. Now are you going to fill it with my tiny body? Let me go and I'll give you three pieces of advice. That way you'll learn if I'm intelligent or stupid."

The hunter agreed to the bird's proposal. However, the bird had one condition. "I will only be able to give you those three pieces of advice if I give you the first one while in your hands, the second from the top of your roof, and the third when I land on the top of that

tree," said the bird to the hunter. The bird also told the hunter that if he followed her advice, he would be blessed with good fortune.

Holding the bird in his hands, the hunter waited for the first piece of advice. "Don't believe something that just can't happen, no matter who says it," said the bird. In order to learn the bird's second piece of advice, the hunter released her from his hands. The bird flew to the roof of the closest house and said,

"Don't cry over spilled milk. If something's over, don't long for it." The hunter waited curiously for the third piece of advice. "Inside me there is a huge pearl unlike any other," said the bird. "That pearl would have brought you and your family prosperity." When the hunter heard this, he began to wail and lament and hit himself.

"Didn't I advise you not to cry over spilled milk?" squawked the bird. However, the hunter continued to mourn the pearl he had lost. Then the bird reminded him of her second piece of advice. "Don't believe something that just can't be, I said. O sir, how could a huge pearl be inside a scrawny, little bird like me?"

The hunter came to his senses and asked curiously what the third piece of advice was.

"You followed the other two so well that now you want a third? Giving advice to an unknowledgeable daydreamer is like sowing seeds in a barren field. That which stupidity and lack of knowledge have ripped cannot be patched. There's no use in my giving you any more advice!" said the bird, and flying away, she disappeared.

Know this: Comprehending something, understanding, learning, and remembering it take intelligence. The mind is what exalts these processes.

The Foolish Bird

One fine day, a hunter, who had gone out to hunt birds in a lush, green meadow, threw a few grain seeds on the ground as bait and retreated behind a bush to wait. The hunter covered himself with green grass and leaves so that he would not be recognized by the birds.

Before long, a bird came, circled around the man, and asked him, "Who are you? What are you doing all dressed up in green like the wild animals in the meadow?"

"I'm a dervish who has renounced the world and is content with grass and weeds," said the hunter. Then the bird saw the seeds of grain on the ground and asked the hunter, "Whose are those?"

"A poor, forlorn orphan entrusted those to me," replied the hunter.

"I am very hungry and weak. Right now, even if that were carrion, I'd eat it. What's to lose, O dervish! Give me permission and let me eat those seeds," the bird begged.

The hunter could see the bird's desperation and impatience. Suddenly, the bird, unable to control itself, leapt upon the seeds and was caught in the hunter's trap. The hunter killed the bird skillfully and set off home. So, the bird paid the price for its haste and lack of self-control.

✦

Know this: When your ambition swells and your desire becomes uncontrollable, you should flee to the One, Whose help is ever sought and cry to Him for assistance.

The Thief and the Villager

One morning, a villager tied a rope around the neck of one of his sheep and set out to market with the sheep following behind him. A clever thief who saw this sneaked up behind the villager, cut the rope and made off with the sheep. Before long, when the villager realized the rope in his hand was slack, he turned around and saw that the rope was cut and his sheep was gone.

As the villager was running around right and left, searching for the thief who had stolen his sheep, he saw a man hanging his head into a well and wailing. Wondering what his plight was, the villager approached the man and asked him, "What happened? Why are you wailing like that?"

The man wailing at the well was none other than the thief who had stolen the villager's sheep. "Don't ask," said the thief. "I dropped a purse containing one hundred gold coins into this well. If you can get it out, I'll gladly give you one fifth of its contents."

Thinking that he could buy exactly ten sheep with one fifth of one hundred gold coins, the villager decided to take on the task. Taking off his clothes so they would not get wet, he climbed into the well. This time, the thief took the man's clothes and disappeared.

The poor villager shouted from the bottom of the well, "There's no purse or anything here!" When there was no response to his call, he climbed out. And what did he see? Neither a man wailing at the well nor the clothes he had left there.

❦

Know this: Greed is a sneaky thief. Like a ghost, it takes on a different form at every breath.

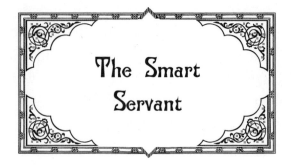

The Smart Servant

Once upon a time, a sultan had a servant as smart as a whip. The sultan gave that servant special attention, gifts and a high salary. However, many in the sultan's court were envious of the salary, which was thirty times more than anyone else's and of the attention their master gave the man.

One day, the other courtiers entered the sultan's presence and said, "How is it that this servant of yours earns the salary of thirty men, when he does not possess the intelligence of thirty?" Announcing that he would give the answer to this question later, the sultan gathered thirty men from his court and took them out to hunt.

While the sultan and his men were hunting, a long caravan of over a hundred camels came into view in the distance. The sultan said to one of the men, "Go and ask which city that caravan is coming from." The man went and asked the leader of the caravan. When he returned, he informed the sultan. "Master, it's coming from the city of Rey."

"And where is it going?" the sultan asked the man. Faced with this question, the man froze and said nothing.

This time the sultan sent another man, commanding him, "Go and ask where the caravan is going." The man rode his horse straight to the caravan, learned where it was going, and rode back to the sultan. "Master, they are going to Yemen," he said. When the sultan asked, "What are they carrying?" that man was surprised and fell silent.

The sultan turned to a third man and said, "Now you go and learn. Let's see what they're carrying." The third man learned that the caravan, while transporting goods of all kinds, was carrying mostly Rey bowls, and informed the sultan of this. However, when the sultan asked,

"When did they leave Rey?" he could not give an answer.

Thirty men rode out and returned in this fashion, yet not one succeeded in gathering all the information for the sultan. Then the sultan tested the servant to whom he gave the salary of thirty men. He too rode out and in one trip gathered all the information concerning the caravan and told the sultan everything he needed to know about it down to the smallest detail.

Turning to his men, the sultan said, "See, this virtuous person is able to accomplish single-handedly what otherwise would require thirty people. However much you thirty men learned by going and returning thirty times, this intelligent person learned all of it in one breath." The courtiers praised the sultan for his justice and agreed that it was indeed a wise decision to attribute so much value to that smart man.

Know this: Whatever loss a person suffers is a result of his inability to work well; whatever profit a person sees is due to his own proper work.

When It Is Too Late

Once, in the dead of night, a band of robbers that sneaked up on a sleeping caravan in an uninhabited desert, stole the caravan's goods by threatening the night guard. The guard, who could not find his voice for fear of their weapons, watched hopelessly as they stole all the goods. When the caravan travelers woke up in the morning and saw that all their goods and camels had been stolen, they surrounded the guard.

"What happened to our goods? Tell us at once," they demanded. "In the night a gang of masked robbers came and made off with everything, right in front of my eyes," answered the guard. "Good gracious! What kind of a guard are you? Why didn't you stand up to the men who took our goods?" exclaimed the caravan travelers. "I was alone. They, however, were a pack of armed men," replied the guard, defending himself. "Well then, since you couldn't oppose them, why didn't you shout and wake us up before the robbers run away?" they asked. "Right as I was about to shout, they threatened me with a knife and told me to be quiet, or else they were going to kill me mercilessly. I was so afraid I clamped my mouth shut," answered the guard.

As the caravan travelers insisted on asking again why he had not shouted, the guard could not stand the pressure any longer and cried, "At that time I'd clamped my mouth shut so tight that I couldn't even breathe, but, if you like, I'll shout all you want now!"

⁂

Know this: After Satan, who disgraces humans, has completely destroyed your life, there's no longer any use in your seeking the aid of God or refuge in Him against Satan's evil influences.

The Trickster Tailor

Once, there was a tailor who was thought to be a trickster. Claiming that the tailor could never cheat him, a self-confident, quick-witted man one evening waged a bet with his friends. If he were to lose the bet, he would give them his thoroughbred stallion, he said.

When the next day dawned, the man, who had been dreaming about how to outwit thieves all night, bought a piece of the most expensive satin and went to the tailor. The tailor showered the man with attention and soon won him over. The man asked the tailor to sew six satin robes for use in battle, the tops narrow and the bottoms wide. Indeed, the man insisted on the robes' shape, saying to the tailor, "They

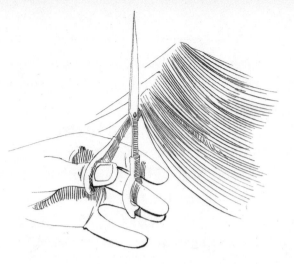

should be wide from the belly down and narrow from the waist up."

The clever tailor began to tell funny stories and jokes and to talk about ancient heroes' feats, lords, swindlers and sharp lads. At the same time, he took out his scissors and began to cut the satin.

The man's sides split with laughter at the tailor's tales. Whenever the laughing man closed his eyes, the tailor tossed a piece of the satin he had cut under the counter. The humor of the stories made the man forget that he had waged a bet and that the tailor was known to be a good cheat. After one joke that the tailor told, the man laughed so hard that he fell to the floor and lay on his back. Seizing this opportunity, the tailor cut another piece of the satin and hid it under his robe by sleight of hand.

As each story ended, the man begged the tailor to tell yet another, and another. As the tailor narrated on, the man was beside himself, lying on the floor, convulsing with laughter. At every opportunity the tailor saw, he cut yet another piece of satin and hid it somewhere. But the man could not get his fill of jokes and stories. In the end, the tailor began to pity the poor man whom he had been able to cheat so well.

The man was demanding, once again, just one more story, when the tailor cut him short. "Enough! If I tell one more ridiculous story, pity upon you! Your robe will be so narrow that you won't be able to fit into it. Is this the time and place to be laughing? If you had any idea what's been going on, you'd be sobbing, not chuckling!"

Know this: The customer is a careless pleasure-seeker who is so intent on listening to the jokes and stories of the tailor, who is the seductive world, that he allows himself to be robbed of the satin, which is his garment for eternity. The tailor of deception steals away your life day by day. Yet, you continually ask him to steal more, saying, 'If only all my days were blessed with fortune!'

The Dervish
and the Judge

O nce upon a time, a man fell ill and was
withering away day by day in his bed. In
order to find a cure for his troubles, he went to
an experienced doctor. The doctor examined the
patient, listened to his heart, and took his pulse,
but, unfortunately, the man was in decline.

The doctor saw the man's hopelessness
and understood that he had only a short time
left to live. He said to the man, "Do whatever
your heart desires so that this illness may pass.
Whatever comes to your mind, do it without
hesitation." Then he warned him, "Hesitation
and abstinence will only increase your illness."

After the examination, the patient obeyed
his heart and went for a walk along the riv-
erside. There, he saw a dervish sitting on the

river bank. The dervish was trying to cool off by washing his hands and feet. Suddenly, the patient felt a strong desire to slap the dervish's bare neck. Remembering the doctor's advice, he decided that he must not forego this desire and —smack!— he delivered a blow to the back of the dervish's neck. The dervish whipped around, and upon seeing the man, became enraged. Dragging the man by his collar, he marched straight to the judge.

When the judge saw the state of the wretched man before the court, he felt sorry for him and decided not to punish him. The judge asked the dervish who had been slapped, "How much money do you have?"

"Only six liras," answered the dervish. "Then spend three liras, and give the other three to this poor man who is sick to death and don't complain," said the judge.

Meanwhile, the sick man was eyeing the judge's head, thinking to himself, "What a handsome neck to slap!" Approaching the judge as if he were going to whisper something private, he waited for the judge to lean forward and then slapped him on the back of the neck. The surprised judge did not know what had hit him.

Before the judge could open his mouth, the sick man said, "Now both of you can be considered my adversaries. Divide the six liras between you. While you fight it out, I'll be on my way." Quickly, he ran away.

As the judge began to fume at the smarting slap, the dervish interrupted, saying, "When I was slapped, you still made me bear the punishment. If your other decisions are like that, what a shame it is!" So, the judge said that in this matter there was no crime and that everything that had happened had occurred beyond their own will. He said that he recognized every blow that might befall him as divinely ordained and sent for his good because every misfortune occurring to the faithful in this life will be amply compensated for in the life to come. "We should submit to pain, to every slap that fate deals us," he advised the dervish.

Know this: The prophets and saints bore whatever suffering came their way without complaint, and those troubles lifted them to higher ranks.

Hidden Treasure

One day, a poor man lost his job and was left helpless. Filled with sorrow, the man prayed to God at every opportunity, saying, "O Lord of lords! O Protector of the wolves and birds! You created me. Grant me a means of sustenance!"

The poor man prayed like this for years. Finally, one night he saw a man in his dreams. This man gave him good news, saying, "Look for your sustenance in the beautifully lettered papers that the papermakers make. Among the papers of your papermaking neighbor is a treasure map. Be the only one to read it and try to find the treasure. Don't give up hope!"

As soon as the man woke up in the morning, he leapt with joy and went immediately to his papermaking neighbor. Glancing at the papers on the floor, the poor man saw one similar to the paper described in his dream, and he shoved it in his pocket. The paper that the man had found really did resemble a treasure map.

On the paper was the following message: "Be assured that there is a treasure outside the city. You know that cupola inside which a martyr is buried. Its back faces the city and its door is directly opposite a meadow. Turn your back to it. Face toward Mecca, place an arrow in your bow and dig where your arrow falls. The treasure is buried there."

By following the map's directions, the man found the cupola, and pulling on his bow with all his strength, he fired an arrow into the distance. Then, he began to dig where his arrow had fallen. The man dug until he was completely exhausted. His pickaxe and shovel both broke, but there was still no trace, no sign of the treasure. Then, he began to dig up the surrounding earth. People watched the man curiously.

The news that the man had found a map of buried treasure traveled as far the sultan's

ears. Seeing as he had not been able to find the treasure, the poor man began to fear that the sultan might harm him. At last, he went and placed the valuable paper in front of the sultan. The man told the sultan that he had dug in several places and that, despite great suffering, he had not been able to find the treasure as he had hoped.

Upon hearing this, the sultan began to have the places where the arrow fell excavated. Hundreds of arrows were shot from the cupola shown on the map, and just as many places were excavated. What a shame it was that not a trace of the treasure was found! Finally, the sultan, who had had the meadows, deserts and mountains dug full of holes, became tired of the whole scheme and angrily threw the treasure map in the man's face.

"This map is befitting of the idle! This task is not one for those who have a proper occupation!" cried the sultan. The poor man was greatly distressed. In desperation he opened up his hands and prayed for a long, long time. After a while, he heard a voice behind him. "You were directed to place an arrow in your bow but not to draw your bow with all your might, as you have been doing. Shoot as gently as possible that the arrow may fall not far from you," said the voice. The man did as he was told, and placing an arrow on the string, made it fly not far.

The arrow fell right by the man's foot. The man, who day after day had followed far-flying arrows and dug in distant spots, this time began to dig in the earth right beneath his own feet. After flinging only a few shovelfuls of dirt, the treasure finally came into view. The man had found the treasure for which he had been searching with so much determination not far away, but rather, right beneath his own feet.

Know this: The further the people in the story shot, the further they were from the treasure. The heart is the center of the self, and God looks at the heart, which is the station of the Lord of all the worlds. In the heart where His name is oft-remembered, the hidden treasury of God is uncovered. God says, 'We are nearer to him than his jugular vein' (Qur'an 50:16). You, however, are shooting your wishes like arrows into the distance.

The Sultan and His Fool

O nce, Sayyid, the sultan of Tirmidh, had an important matter to take care of in Samarqand, and he began to look for a courier who could get there within three to four days. An imperial edict was sent in every direction, announcing the need for a courier who could quickly reach Samarqand riding the sultan's fastest horse. It was also announced that the person who succeeded at this task would be given a large sum of money and gifts. Now, the sultan had a fool named Dalqak. Dalqak, who heard the sultan's edict while out in the coun-tryside, readied a fine horse and rode straight to Tirmidh.

Two horses dropped dead of exhaustion under his whip before Dalqak, covered with

dust, arrived at the palace at midnight. He immediately demanded an audience with the sultan. Great curiosity and panic spread in the palace. Even the sultan was curious about Dalqak's behavior and gave in to conjecture. The city's inhabitants wondered what the message to be delivered for the sultan at this time of night could be, and they were afraid of a calamity. Rumors spread that a secret enemy or a deadly disaster was on the way.

"Seeing that Dalqak rode two royal horses into the ground, it must be something very important," they whispered to each other. Those who knelt on their knees in bitter sorrow, those who groaned and lamented, and those who fearfully predicted disorder and disaster managed to turn the whole city into a mourning square. The people who asked Dalqak could not get any answer. Indicating that he needed more time to catch his breath, Dalqak answered their curious questions by making a sign for silence, but this only increased their curiosity and anxiety.

Finally, Dalqak was summoned by the sultan. He entered into the presence of the sultan and greeted him, kissing the ground. The sultan, who was becoming even more anxious than the people, cried, "Tell me quickly! What has happened? Why all this haste and excitement?" Dalqak replied, "I am very tired. I changed my horse several times to come here. Please give me permission to rest."

The sultan waited for a while, but his tongue and the roof of his mouth grew dry with nerves and foreboding. Seeing Dalqak, one of his most faithful men, and the one who had always entertained him and made him laugh, in this state deeply affected the sultan. Fearful of merciless enemies' attacks or other disasters to come, the sultan could no longer wait. He burst out, "Tell me quickly! What happened? What's going on? Who caused you to come here like this? Why do you look so wretched?" Dalqak replied, "In the village I heard that our sultan had announced by the town-crier in every district that he would grant a large sum of money and gifts to the person who could ride to Samarqand and back in three days."

"Yes!" exclaimed the sultan. "I came here as fast as I could, because I wanted to tell you that I will not be able to do it," said Dalqak "What!" gasped the sultan. "I don't have the strength or the quickness to do that. You shouldn't trust me with this matter or set your hopes on me," continued Dalqak. "Alas, may God give you what you deserve! You spread fear in the city and sent everyone into a complete frenzy. Why was so much haste necessary for such a small thing?" exclaimed the sultan.

Then, he gave Dalqak a good scolding for making so much disturbance about nothing. The sultan's men, who still surmised that Dalqak was hiding something and that he was not willing to tell the truth, tried to scare him into talking by using force and subjecting him to all kinds of torture. Dalqak escaped from this torture with great difficulty and learned a good lesson about the consequences of unnecessary behavior.

༺ ❖ ༻

Know this: If the heart is a mouth, idle talk is like mockery coming from it. True words are clear and calm the heart. The heart is not calmed by untrue or idle words.

The Camel, the Ox, and the Ram

Once upon a time, a camel, an ox and a ram found a bundle of grass on the path they were traveling. The ram sprang forward and said, "If we divide this among ourselves, none of us will fill our stomachs. Isn't it best if the oldest one of us eats this bundle of grass?"

The ox and the camel found the ram's proposal favorable, and they decided to calculate their ages. All three of them agreed, saying, "Let each of us tell when our lives began. Let's see which of us is the oldest. When this becomes clear, we'll be quiet."

The ram spoke first. "I've been grazing since the days of Ishmael's sacrificial ram," he said and

claimed to be the oldest animal. "No, I'm the oldest," said the ox. "I was one of the pair of oxen that the Prophet Adam drove. The forefather of all humans, the Prophet Adam, plowed the earth and sowed seed, you know. I was paired with his other ox."

When the camel heard what the ox and ram were saying, he quickly lowered his head, bit into the bundle of grass on the ground and, without saying a word, lifted it into the air and began eating it. As the ox and the ram watched the camel in utter surprise, the camel said, "I don't need to give you a date. Since I have such a great body and such a long neck, I don't need any other proof!"

Know this: The only purpose of the apparently reasonable arguments of the ox and the ram was to dupe their companions so they could have all the food. The camel, who understood that and was not impressed, taught them a lesson. What are the earth's nooks and crannies compared with the vastness of the sky?

The Mouse and the Frog

Once upon a time, a mouse and a frog met on the bank of a creek and became friends. These two friends, who met every day and enjoyed themselves by sharing stories, wanted to visit each other's home. Unfortunately, because one of them lived in the depths of the water and the other on land, such visits were impossible.

One day, the mouse complained to the frog, "O beacon of intelligence, whenever I come to tell you something, I see you splashing around in the water and I can't reach you. I can't dive into the water because I was made to live on the land. So, I can't speak loud enough to make you hear me."

The two friends looked for ways to see each other whenever they wanted and tried to find a solution to their problem. At last, they decided to get a piece of string and communicate with one another by means of it. The mouse said, "One end must be tied to your waist and the other to me, your partner. This way, we two may be united whenever we want to see each other and be fastened together like body and soul."

Whenever the mouse wanted to see the frog, he pulled his end of the string. The frog, too, expressed his desire to meet by tugging on the other end of the string. Days, then months passed by. The two friends satisfied their longing by this communication system, meeting up whenever they wished.

One day, a spotted crow circling in the sky noticed the mouse. He quickly dived down and, as soon as he had caught the mouse, took to the air again. As the crow rose into the air, the frog on the other end of the string was also pulled out of the water and became airborne. The people who saw this sight had no idea what was going on and cried in amazement, "How in the world did that crow manage to take a frog from the depths of the water into its mouth and fly?"

❦

Know this: The frog is the soul in the water of ecstatic bliss. Away from the mouse, which is the body, it would remain at peace in its water. However, it attaches itself to the mouse, which lives on dry land and which drags it from the water of bliss with that string.

Sultan Mahmud
and the Thieves

One night, as Sultan Mahmud was strolling alone, he came across a band of thieves. The thieves, not recognizing him, asked him who he was and why he was out at that time of night. Sultan Mahmud said to the thieves, "I am one of you." One of the thieves sprang forward and said, "Come on, let each of us tell what talent he possesses. Let's see." Each of the thieves described his talent and demonstrated his skill.

One of them declared, "All my talent lies in my eyes. Whomever I see in the dark of the night, I recognize him by day, too." Another one said, "O, you sellers of skills, my talent lies in my two ears. When a dog barks, I understand what it is saying." Attaching small value to hearing

in comparison with sight, the thieves laughed, "That's worth less than two cents out of a hundred bucks!" Another thief boasted, "My talent is in my arms. With the strength of my arms, I can make great holes in anything."

"My talent lies in my nose. My job is to find out how much money is above and below the earth by smelling it," said another thief. "My talent is in my hands. I can throw a lasso to the peak of a mountain," declared another.

Now it was the sultan's turn. The thieves turned to him and asked, "What is your talent?" The sultan turned to the thieves and answered, "My talent lies in my beard. Thanks to my beard, criminals are freed from punishment." The thieves could not hide their curiosity about this answer. Sultan Mahmud continued his explanation, saying, "When criminals have been handed over to the executioners, I stroke my beard and save them from the executioners' blades. If I take pity and stroke my beard, they won't kill them."

When the thieves heard Sultan Mahmud's remarks, they cried, "You are our chief. In hard times we'll be saved, thanks to you." Then they all set out together. Sultan Mahmud said, "Since I'm your chief, follow me," and led them all together along the road toward the sultan's palace.

As they approached the palace, they heard a dog barking. The thief who understood dogs' language listened carefully to the bark and said, "The dog says that the sultan is among us." Another thief, smelling the earth, said, "This is the property of a widow." After continuing on a bit, he said, "This is the property of the sultan, where he keeps his treasure."

The lasso-throwing thief threw a lasso onto a tall wall and began climbing. The hole-making thief let the other thieves in by punching a hole into the wall. The thieves stole gold pieces, silver- and gold-embroidered cloths and valuable jewels from the sultan's treasury and hid the loot elsewhere.

Disguising himself like an expert, the sultan learned and memorized the places where the thieves stayed, their names and their appearances. Secretly, he returned to his palace, and in the morning he told his courtiers what had happened. Immediately, soldiers went and arrested the thieves and brought them before the sultan.

With their hands bound, the thieves began to tremble in the presence of the sultan. However, as they stood in front of his throne, the thief who quickly recognized anyone he had seen at night knew the sultan as soon as he saw him. As his eye was the knower of the sultan, he thought, "This one was with us last night, our fellow night wanderer and companion. He was seeing our actions and hearing our secrets.

I will implore his grace for me and my fellows, since he will never turn away his face from him that knew him." Then, he began to plead, "O Sultan of hidden journeys, now is the time to be kind and benevolently stroke your beard. Each one of us demonstrated his talent, but all those talents have only increased our bad luck. Please, rescue us!"

The sultan realized that the thieves had learned a great lesson from those events, and with a stroke of his beard, he commanded the executioners bringing the thieves to the execution stand to set them free.

❦

Know this: He whose eyes see God in the world is safe from destruction. The thief is like the one who knows God, without Whose mercy no sinner is saved. His plea for mercy is a prayer to God. That one could be the intercessor for faults because his eye did not wander from the sultan and recognized him without fail when he saw him by day. The most important sense, higher than all the other senses, is the immediate recognition of the Divine. O You Who sees us in the day and in the night! We cannot see You, for our eyes have been veiled.

The Three Princes

A long time ago, a sultan had three sons, each of whom was as brave, as generous, and as intelligent as the next. In order to learn about the country their father ruled and to bring order to the cities' affairs, the three princes agreed to set out on a long journey. As the princes bade farewell to the sultan by kissing his hand, he advised them to go everywhere except to a certain castle known as "The Robber of Reason," so as to avoid the danger and trials they would fall into there. He told them to stay far away from the castle, which was covered from top to bottom with captivating pictures. Of course, if the princes' father had not given them this warning, they would not have even dreamed of the castle. However, the sultan's warning cast a deep doubt in the

princes' hearts, and the forbidden nature of the castle only increased their desire to see it.

The princes immediately headed for the castle about which they were so curious, and finally they arrived there. The entire castle was decorated with pictures. The castle had five gates which opened to the sea and land. The princes were astounded by the castle's thousands of pictures and paintings.

One painting was especially captivating, and all three of them stood daydreaming excitedly in front of it. The princes, who had fallen in love with the painting, began to ask whose likeness it was. They asked an old man they came across at the castle. When the old man answered, "This painting is the portrait of a Chinese sultan's daughter, for whose sake many admirers have burned with great passion," their fascination grew all the more.

Finally, the princes decided to travel to China in order to find the Chinese sultan's daughter. When they arrived in China, they hid in a place near the sultan's palace. After a while, the oldest prince became impatient and proposed to his brothers that they go ahead and venture out into the open and enter into the sultan's presence. However, the middle prince and the youngest prince warned him to wait just a little longer. Paying no heed to their warning and acting on impulse, the oldest brother went to find the hidden beloved in the palace, where he entered into the sultan's presence and confided his troubles to him.

Yet, the sultan, who had long since learned from his men about the princes' entrance into China and their intentions, had already taken the necessary precautions. The oldest of the princes did not return from the sultan's palace. Sensing the death of his older brother, the middle prince, whose younger brother had fallen ill, set out alone for the palace to attend the funeral. When the sultan saw another member of the same family before him, he found a way to kill him, too. Soon, only the third prince remained.

Fortunately, this last prince understood what was going on—that the portrait that had captivated them so much was actually a trap laid by the Chinese sultan—and he quickly left the palace and returned home to his father.

Know this: Those who sell valueless wares which resemble nothing true confuse minds with all their extravagant displays.

Omar the Generous

Once, a poor man was unable to pay back the loan of nine thousand gold pieces which he had taken from a friend. Now, living in Tabriz was a man named Badraddin Omar who was known for his generosity. Strangers and poor people would come to Omar to borrow money. It was said that he turned no one away and fulfilled every request.

The poor man truly believed that he would find the solution to his problem and that he would be able to pay off his debt with Omar's help. The man found Badraddin Omar's house and knocked on the door. But alas, the people in the house said that Omar had passed away!

When the man heard this, he screamed and fainted. The people around him poured rose-water on this stranger who had fainted and col-

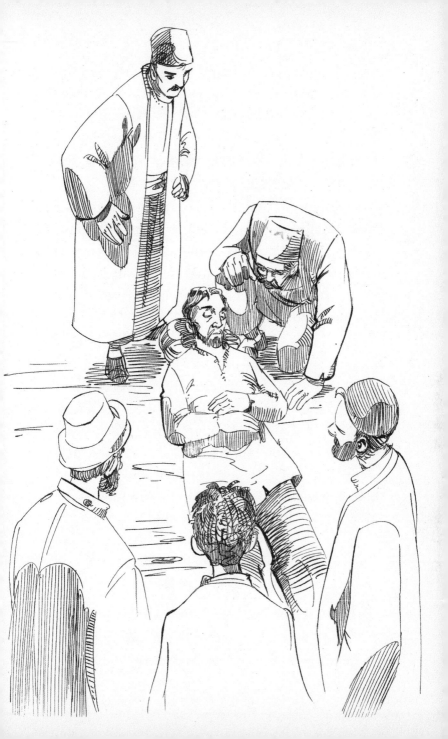

lapsed on the ground, and tried to console him. All the poor man's hopes had been dashed. Even though Badraddin Omar's assistant, who heard about the man, tried to help him by collecting money from the public, he could not collect nearly enough.

Badraddin Omar's assistant and the poor man finally went to the philanthropist's grave and prayed. The two desperate men returned home exhausted and, after eating supper, fell into a deep sleep. That night, the assistant saw his master in a dream.

Badraddin pitied the poor man's indebtedness and wanted him to be helped. In the dream, Badraddin described to his assistant where he had buried some very valuable jewels and ordered the poor man's debt to be paid with those jewels. In the morning, the assistant went to the place where the jewels were buried and dug them up. By selling the unique jewels, he paid off the poor man's debt.

Know this: Giving alms never decreases your property; on the contrary, generosity and good deeds protect your property from disappearing.

The Flawed Horse

Long ago, there was a gentleman who owned a beautiful, thoroughbred steed. Even among the horses in the sultan's stable there was no creature as magnificent. One day, the gentleman mounted his horse and went to a ceremony which the sultan would attend. The sultan noticed the beautiful thoroughbred horse among all the others. The horse's dignified trot and its color caught the sultan's eye, and he began to ask questions about the steed which had charmed him. When he learned that it belonged to a gentleman of his lands, he commanded his men to bring the animal to his palace.

The soldiers immediately went to the gentleman's home, seized the horse and took it to the palace. The poor gentleman, try as he might,

could not stomach the seizure of his beloved horse and, like a wilting flower, began to wither away with grief. He confided his troubles to the sultan's vizier, requested help from him and promised that he would give up all his capital in exchange for the horse.

The vizier was an expert at influencing the sultan. He promised the gentlemen that he would get back his horse and entered into the sultan's presence. Right at that very moment, the sultan was busy admiring the horse's beauty and gazing at it in fascination. Seeing his vizier approach, the sultan praised the horse, exclaiming, "Vizier, look at this thoroughbred steed! Isn't it beautiful? It's as if it was not born on earth, but rather came from Heaven!"

The vizier understood the sultan's intention and, in order to discourage him, replied, "O Sultan of Sultans, your heart's desire makes the devil look like an angel to you." As the sultan was pondering this reply, the vizier continued his argument, "If you look carefully, you'll see that this horse is very attractive. But its head doesn't fit its body. This horse's head is flawed. It's almost like an ox's head."

Upon hearing the vizier's remark, the sultan looked carefully at the horse's head and really did find it ugly. The moment the sultan saw the fault in the horse which he had previously been observing with such admiration, he decided against keeping it and ordered it to be sent back to its owner.

Know this: O sure one, this fleeting world is like a dry and rotten walnut; just look at it from afar without trying to sniff it.

The Treasure

A long time ago in Baghdad, an heir squandered away his entire fortune and was left without a penny in his pocket. The man knocked on the door of every person he knew and did not know, asking for help, but no one came to his aid. One night, the heir saw a man in his dream.

The man in the dream described the location of a treasure in Egypt and advised him to go there. As soon as the heir woke up in the morning, he left Baghdad for Egypt. However, he was not far along the road before he found he had no provisions and only rags for clothes. He waited for the night in order to beg.

Even though the heir begged until midnight, he was not able to get any alms. Near dawn, the poor man, who had not found any food, was searching for a place to rest, when suddenly a night watchman appeared in front of him. Thinking that the man was a thief, the watchman gave him a good beating. The heir suffered countless wounds to his body. He begged the watchman to give him the opportunity to explain who he was. "Alright, I'll give you a break. Come on and tell me! What were you doing outside at night? Tell me! Let's see!" said the watchman.

The heir swore to tell the truth and explained who he was, insisting that he was not a thief. He stated that he had come to Egypt from Baghdad. In order to save himself, the poor man also related the dream he had seen and revealed why he had come to Egypt. As the heir spoke, the watchman's excitement and interest grew. Finally, the watchman's eyes grew moist and his tears began to flow. The heir could not understand why he was crying.

"You're not a thief or a bad person, but you're quite foolish!" cried the watchman. "Falling fancy to a dream, you came here all the way from Baghdad! As for me, how many times have I seen a treasure in Baghdad in my dreams." The

heir was very surprised at what the watchman said. The watchman continued, "A man I saw in my dreams said, 'In Baghdad there is a treasure buried in a man's house. Go and find it!' But I haven't budged an inch from here. But you, you get carried away by a dream and come here."

The heir's astonishment grew even more because the person in the watchman's dream was none other than himself. That meant that the treasure was buried at his house in Baghdad. "Why did I suffer poverty in vain, when the treasure was in my house the whole time?" said the man.

After a long journey, he returned to Baghdad. Digging in his own garden, he found the treasure he had desired, and the prosperity he had searched for, near the base of a tree.

Know this: There are many careless people who set out to get ahead and to acquire more goods and property. Their actions become the cause of their own deaths. Whatever they leave behind becomes the share of others.

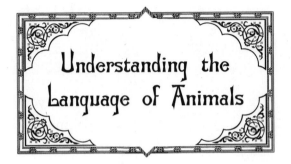

Understanding the Language of Animals

One day, a man came before the Prophet Moses and said, "Teach me the language of the animals so that I can understand them and learn various lessons." Moses tried to get the man to give up this idea by talking about the many dangers it entailed. However, the man was stuck on the idea and kept on repeating his request. Moses warned the man that he might encounter trouble, but the man wanted, if nothing else, to be able to understand the conversations of his rooster and his dog.

Finally, the Prophet Moses prayed to God, asking Him to grant this man the ability to understand what his rooster and his dog were saying. Moses' prayer was accepted, and he gave the man the good news. The next morning, in

order to try out his new ability, the man came
to the threshold of his door and waited. As his
maid shook out the tablecloth, a piece of stale
bread fell to the ground. The rooster immediately snatched up the single piece of bread.

The dog sprang forward and bellowed, "You
are treating me unjustly! You can eat pieces of

wheat. I, however, cannot eat any grain. I'm in a terrible state. You, who can eat wheat, barley or other grain, snatched this one piece of bread which was my lot! You tread on dogs' rights!"

The rooster replied to the dog, "Be quiet! Quit sulking! In return for this God will give you other things. Your master's horse is going to suffer an injury. Don't be sad. Tomorrow you'll eat lots and lots of meat. The horse's death means a holiday for you dogs. You'll get all kinds of sustenance without even lifting a paw."

When the man, who was listening to the animals from behind the doorpost, heard these words, he immediately took his horse to the market and sold it. As a result, the rooster felt rather embarrassed when he saw the dog again.

The next day, when the rooster again snatched a piece of bread, the dog accused him of lying and tyranny. "Hey, I thought you said the horse was going to be injured!" the dog barked sarcastically. "The horse was injured, but somewhere else," crowed the rooster. "Our master managed to escape any financial loss by selling the horse. He passed the damage onto someone else. However, tomorrow his mule is going to be injured. There will be a feast for the dogs." When the man heard this, he immediately sold his mule, too.

On the third day, when the dog saw that the mule had also been sold, he turned to the rooster and scolded him, saying, "You, bird-brained, fickle-feathered liar! What about everything you said?" The rooster replied, "He sold the mule, but tomorrow his slave is going to die, and his relatives will distribute bread to the dogs and the beggars."

When the man heard these words, he ran and sold his slave, and since he had escaped any financial loss, he breathed a sigh of relief. Thankful for having experienced all these events, he declared happily, "I have escaped three disasters in this world." The man, who could understand what his dog and rooster were saying, was overjoyed that he would be able to avoid any future disasters in the same manner.

The rooster, whose predictions had made him look like a liar three times in a row, was now very embarrassed when he met the dog. "How much longer are you going to tell me lies? Don't you know how to tell anything else but lies?" sneered the dog.

The roster crowed at the dog who was denigrating him so, "God forbid I should tell a lie! We roosters take no part in lies. We roosters tell the truth, just like the muezzin who calls Muslims to prayer. We observe the sun and wait for the right time. God gave us the gift of communicating the morning prayer time to humans. What we say is always true. The slave died near the man to whom he was sold. Our master managed to save his capital, but in doing so, he shed his own blood. Tomorrow, he himself will definitely die. The heirs who will mourn him will sacrifice an ox. Tomorrow, you're going to receive all kinds of blessings. Meat and bread will be given out."

When the master heard the rooster's remarks, he became feverish and ran huffing and puffing to the Prophet Moses. "O Prophet! Come to my rescue! Save me from this end!" he groaned. However, it was too late. The next morning the man died. His heirs distributed abundant amounts of food to the poor, to the beggars and to the animals at their homes.

❧ ❋ ❧

Know this: Bodily injury and loss of property are beneficial for the soul. They save man from sin. Be sure of this.

The Teacher's Fear

O ne day among many days, the children at a school became tired of studying and being tormented by their teacher. Gathering together, they began to work out various schemes of how not to go to school. "If only our teacher were sick and we could escape this torment for a few days. That way we'd get away from the boredom of this prison, even if just for a little while," they were saying, when one of them had a brilliant idea.

As soon as the teacher entered the class-room, she suggested, she would approach him and say, "Teacher, why are you so yellow? You don't look well at all. Either you've caught a bad cold, or you've got malaria!" Then, thirty children were to say the same thing to the teacher, one by one. The teacher, unable to tolerate so many remarks, would probably call off class and send the students home. In this way, the children were going to send their teacher home and escape from lessons and school. The children swore not to tell their secret and not to go back on their word.

In the morning, as soon as the teacher entered the classroom for the first lesson, one of the children sprang forward and cried, "I hope there is nothing wrong, teacher. Your face is so yellow and haggard!"

"I don't have any aches or pains," said the teacher. "Go and sit in your seat. Don't talk nonsense!" he scolded the child. Yet, despite his insistence that nothing was wrong with him, a slight feeling of fear began to grow in the teacher's heart.

Before long, a second child came up and said to the teacher, "I hope you feel better soon, teacher. You look really pale and jaundiced." The other children came up after him and, one by one, told the teacher how sick he was. The teacher's sense of doubt grew, and the poor man began to think that he really was sick. He became angry at his wife, who had

sent him off to school that morning without even noticing his illness, and began to wonder if she really loved him.

The teacher, who now really was beginning to feel tired and ill, suddenly set out for his home. All of the children followed him. When the teacher reached home, his wife exclaimed, "My goodness! Why have you come so early? Did something bad happen? May God protect us!" The poor man, who now really believed that he was sick, said to his wife, "Are you blind? Look at the color of my face! Look at me! Even strangers, noticing my illness, have offered their sympathy, yet you're not even concerned about me!" Even though his wife replied, "There's nothing wrong with you. This fear is groundless and ridiculous," she could not convince him. The man said he was trembling violently and, repeating that his face was jaundiced, he got into bed and began to moan and groan.

Faking sad expressions, his pupils sat down at his bedside and began to study their lessons. The smart child who had come up with this whole scheme warned her friends to be quiet now. "Our voices make the teacher's head hurt," she yelled. When the teacher heard this, he told the girl she was right and sent the children home.

While returning to their homes, the children congratulated each other gleefully, clapping their hands. However, they could not make their mothers believe that the teacher really was sick. Their mothers and fathers, who doubted what their children had told them, went to visit the teacher in his home that very morning. The teacher was lying under his blankets and covers, still continuing to shake.

Know this: If a person has his mind set on something, he cannot think of anything else; in fact, he'll continue along regardless of what is true or what others say.